Brief Notes

MARKETING

The publications in *Brief Notes* are outlines of core topics of interest to professionals involved in shopping center management. The outlines are capsule overviews of each topic. Many key points are covered, and shopping center examples are provided for further illustration. Core concepts in each area guide you on topics you may want to explore further. Each outline also contains a helpful glossary.

Brief Notes is designed to provide a helpful and informative overview of the topics covered. It is not intended to be a substitute for more extensive learning that can be achieved through attending ICSC educational programs and reading additional ICSC professional publications.

The outlines contained in *Brief Notes: Shopping Center Management:*

- Management Overview
- Finance
- Insurance and Risk Management
- The Lease and Its Language
- Leasing Strategies
- Maintenance
- Marketing
- Retailing
- Security

Brief Notes

MARKETING

ICSC International Council of Shopping Centers
New York

ABOUT THE INTERNATIONAL COUNCIL OF SHOPPING CENTERS

The International Council of Shopping Centers (ICSC) is the trade association of the shopping center industry. Serving the shopping center industry since 1957, ICSC is a not-for-profit organization with over 44,000 members in 77 countries worldwide.

ICSC members include shopping center

- owners
- developers
- managers
- marketing specialists
- leasing agents
- retailers
- researchers
- attorneys

- architects
- contractors
- consultants
- investors
- lenders and brokers
- academics
- public officials

ICSC sponsors more than 200 meetings a year and provides a wide array of services and products for shopping center professionals, including deal making events, conferences, educational programs, accreditation, awards, publications and research data.

For more information about ICSC, write or call the
International Council of Shopping Centers
1221 Avenue of the Americas
New York, NY 10020-1099
Telephone: 646-728-3800
Fax: 212-589-5555
info@icsc.org
http://www.icsc.org

This publication is designed to provide accurate and authoritative information in regard to the subject matter covered. It is sold with the understanding that the publisher is not engaged in rendering legal, accounting, or other professional services. If legal advice or other expert assistance is required, the services of a competent professional person should be sought.

> —*From a Declaration of Principles jointly adopted by a Committee of the American Bar Association and a Committee of Publishers.*

Companies, professional groups, clubs and other organizations may qualify for special terms when ordering quantities of more than 20 of this title.

Published by
International Council of Shopping Centers
Publications Department
1221 Avenue of the Americas
New York, NY 10020-1099
ICSC Catalog No.: 242
ISBN: 1-58268-028-0

Contents

Preface

Marketing is both a strategy and a method for bringing a product or service to the attention of prospective customers. When an entire shopping center is the "product," a variety of approaches can be successful in creating and maintaining an appropriate image to inform and attract consumers.

With the increasing sophistication of shoppers and the proliferation of centers of all sizes and types, competition for consumer disposable income is more intense than ever. The more consumers spend in retail stores and restaurants in a shopping center, the higher those retailers will sell per square foot of space. Higher sales per square foot almost always translate into higher rent per square foot for the landlord that leases retail space based on demand by retailers. This means that effective marketing of a shopping center is critical to its current performance and to its vitality in the future.

An effective marketing plan is the foundation for the successful promotion of any shopping center. The plan requires a commitment from the center's landlord and ongoing support from all parties connected with the center. The marketing plan must be a working tool for the entire staff. It should be easily accessible, regularly monitored, reevaluated quarterly and updated annually.

This book guides you—the shopping center professional—through the fundamental parts of a shopping center marketing plan. Terms and concepts are clearly defined in the glossary.

Acknowledgments

The material in this outline is based in part on a course presented at the International Council of Shopping Centers (ICSC) John T. Riordan School for Professional Development Management, Marketing and Leasing Institutes.

The International Council of Shopping Centers gratefully acknowledges the individuals mentioned below, who have contributed their expertise to this publication.

Johnna Van Deurzen, CMD, CLS, General Growth Properties, Inc.
Garnet E. Vaughan, SCMD, Principal, The Marketing Department

THE BASICS OF MARKETING

Marketing is the process of getting your product into the hands of the consumer, and its application varies from shopping center to shopping center.

Marketing is important to everyone involved in a shopping center. To be specific:

- Landlords want to maximize the center's value. The marketing director's role is a most important role because it impacts the shopping center's net operating income and enhances tenant relations. In addition, managers who are well versed in marketing increase their growth potential as ownership asks managers to handle more and more responsibility.

- Managers, with the owner's goals in mind, want to increase the center's net operating income (NOI) through increased rents and percentage rents and sponsorship income. Effective marketing increases tenant retail sales and landlord income. They know that satisfied tenants are a center's best ambassadors when it comes to sharing positive information with new prospects.

- Tenants want to see increased traffic and sales that generate income for them.

The Marketing Plan

The cornerstone of an effective marketing program is the marketing plan, which acts as a guide. A marketing plan is a written document that addresses the needs of the shopping center in a logical sequence and includes a commitment to the goals of the center as a whole. The marketing plan works as an integral part of the center's business plan. Many companies have an established format that is used by all their shopping centers. The major elements of the shopping center five-step marketing plan are:

- Situation analysis
- Problems/Opportunities
- Goals/Objectives
- Strategies
- Tactics

The benefits of the marketing plan include:

- Identifying the strengths and weaknesses of a particular shopping center when compared to the competition.

- Defining what sets a center apart from others.
- Identifying trends in the market area, national retail arena and changes in the behavior, beliefs and shopping habits of customers.
- Setting a common goal by merging the interests of tenants, landlords and management.
- Arranging priorities by listing objectives in order of importance.
- Building credibility for management and marketing by demonstrating that a plan was developed in advance, and set in writing, to guide the process and focus energy in the right areas.
- Establishing a comprehensive and well-integrated process to increase revenue for the shopping center through goals-setting, strategies and tactics that go beyond marketing to leasing, development, operational and other disciplines that enhance center productivity.

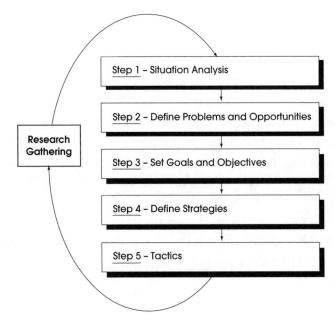

Core Concepts

✓ Methods for accumulating primary research

✓ Sources of secondary research and how to interpret them

✓ Internal data, e.g., sales reports, occupancy rates

✓ Understanding competitive climate

SITUATION ANALYSIS

Research is the foundation of a marketing plan and the gathering of data is ongoing throughout the marketing process. It also occurs before the first step of the marketing plan (analysis of the situation) and after the fifth step of the marketing plan (tactics implementation). The marketing plan process is a continuous circle in which research follows the fifth step to start the plan all over again. You must have information about your trade area, your competition, your center and your consumers in order to develop an appropriate plan. Be thorough—the plan is only as good as the information you bring into the Situation Analysis.

Primary Research

There are primary and secondary sources of information.

Primary research is information you gather via:

- **Intercept interviews**—surveys of shoppers while they are at the center, particularly when they are exiting. These interviews, which should include a minimum of 300 shoppers, are a means of gathering residents' zip codes or postal codes and demographic data as well as information about their shopping habits. The place-of-residence information gathered through these surveys is used to define your trade area, including primary, secondary and inflow.
- **Telephone surveys** of residents within your trade area
- **Focus groups** can be an effective way of gathering a large amount of information, usually in-depth insight on how your market feels on a specific topic. They offer perceptions that are not statistically reliable.
- **Survey cards** used to evaluate a special event can collect zip codes, demographics or customer opinions about the event.
- **Internal reports** are useful in determining your center's performance matrix. This includes tenant sales reports, occupancy costs, rental income, and traffic counters (both pedestrian and vehicles).

Secondary Research

Secondary research is information not gathered firsthand. Some of the best sources include:

- Census information
- Chambers of commerce

- Local magazines or newspapers
- Libraries
- Gas, phone, electric companies
- Department/anchor stores
- Universities
- Mailing lists from your own center's tenants (may be used to gather their customers' zip and postal codes)
- Residential real estate sales representatives (they know the average home sale price and turnover rate for the surrounding community).
- Trade magazines
- City, county, state or province and federal Department of Commerce
- Bureau of Economic Analysis
- National retail trends (icsc.org, nrf.com)
- Trade Web site information

Updating Your Research

Do your primary research, such as a shopper intercept survey, telephone survey and focus groups, every two or three years or whenever a major shift occurs in your market area. New research is called for when, for example:

- Your center has changed significantly (i.e., tenant mix, anchor store relocation, a renovation has been completed).
- A new roadway is built near your center.
- A major employer closes.
- A new housing development opens.
- Another shopping center is constructed in your area.
- An anchor is considered to be added to your center
- A redevelopment of your center is considered

Define Your Trade Area

You must know where your shoppers live. In most cases the home zip or postal codes of shoppers will help define your area. Some smaller centers may have a trade area that is smaller than the zip or postal code area. In cases like this, definition would be specified by census tract information drawn from customer street addresses.

Residence information is gathered typically through interviewing shoppers at the center (intercept interviews). Once your trade area is defined you must conduct a situation analysis before identifying your center's strengths and weaknesses and prior to setting objectives. Key questions to ask when collecting data for your situation analysis follow:

- What are the major industries in your area? Are layoffs or major changes planned? What rhythms do they follow? For example, if your area's major employer issues paychecks on the fifteenth and last day of each month, your center can time marketing and sales events accordingly.
- What major roadways run close to the center? Any changes expected?
- Are there any natural boundaries (for example, mountains or rivers) that close off your market area?
- How do shoppers reach your center?
- What is unique about your trade area? For example, a nearby university may contribute a large student population.
- Where are your competing centers located? What is unique about their anchors and tenant mix?

Find Out Who Your Shoppers Are

You need the following information:

- Demographic: Basic statistics about the shoppers in your trade area, including age, gender, annual household income, education level, occupation, size of household, makeup of household (children or no children), and zip or postal codes
- Behavioral: How your shoppers behave while in your center. For example: When do they shop? Do they eat? How far do they drive to get to your center? What is the average number of annual visits? Buyer conversion can also be very revealing—when your shoppers visit stores in the center, how many leave those stores without making a purchase? More important, what is the percentage of stores visited where purchases were made (where browsers were converted into buyers)?
- Psychographic: This includes lifestyle issues such as how people are influenced and how they spend their money. Two families with the same demographic profiles can be very different psychographically. For example, two neighboring households, each made up of college-educated parents, with two children per family and household incomes of more than $100,000 per year, may use their dollars differently.

Family A may have a recreational vehicle in their driveway and a sailboat and a mountain bike for each family member. Family B may have built a media center in their basement, be very active in the community and enjoy entertaining at home. Each family will relate very differently to your shopping center. You can expect Family A to be away on weekends and do their shopping during the week, while Family B might very well pay a weekend visit to your center. While there, what each family chooses to buy will be influenced by lifestyles as well as demographics. There are currently several software programs available to identify pertinent psychographic information about your center's shoppers and the trade area residents.

Study Your Center

To create a successful marketing program, you should think of your center as a "product." You must know it and have a thorough understanding of what benefits your center—the product—offers the shopper and how it differs from the competition.

Because you are very familiar with your center, you may not see it objectively. Try the following:

- Get the opinions of people who are not at the center as often as you are.
- Vary your perceptions, for example, by occasionally driving a different route to the center or by entering the center from different entrances each time you arrive.
- Walk around the center frequently. Ask a different observer—for example, a maintenance worker, security officer or leasing agent—to accompany you and point out what you may not be seeing or hearing.
- Know the significant internal or external issues for the property and the trade area.

Because your center is your product, you should examine its "packaging." For example, the building—your product's box—must be in excellent condition, signage—your product's label—must be visible and legible, sidewalks should be swept, entrance doors should open easily, interior doors should be clean, the areas around the center's trash receptacles should be free of litter and restrooms should have ample supplies of paper and be clean and very presentable.

Your product must also be accessible. Identify any obstacles that might keep customers away. For example, are driving lanes wide enough and parking areas sufficiently accessible to shopping? In a store, do crowded aisles or awkward freestanding displays come between a shopper and a potential purchase?

In analyzing your shopping center's physical and visual attributes, you should also check out:

- Physical structure of the property (age, signage, maintenance history, etc.)
- Traffic flow and access
- Signage issues
- Landscaping
- Sponsorship and/or charitable partnerships
- Restaurant/food selection
- Specialty leasing
- Security perceptions
- Parking issues
- Common area maintenance (CAM) and real estate taxes (RET) tenant costs compared to your competition
- Shopper amenities offered—soft play, valet parking, family restrooms, soft seating, etc.

You should also know and analyze the performance of your center and its merchants. At the minimum, have the following information for referral:

- Date/year the center opened
- Date/year the center was renovated/expanded
- GLA (gross leasable area square footage excluding anchors that own their own stores)
- Total Retail Area (GLA plus anchors that own their own stores)

- Department Stores—square footage and sales volume of each
- List of key specialty shops—often called focus or sparkle merchants
- Merchandise mix—product and price point represented as well as voids in the mix
- Current year sales per square foot
- Next year's projected sales per square foot
- Sales distribution by month
- Sales distribution by merchandise category
- Sales distribution by location within the center
- Current year overage rent income
- Next year's projected overage rent income
- Rent spreads between new and expiring leases
- Tenant occupancy costs percentages
- Current year occupancy rate
- Next year's projected occupancy rate
- Anticipated vacancies/bankruptcies (watch for high occupancy costs, receivable challenges, kick-out clauses)
- Department store stability
- Lease expirations for the next three years (is a big "roll" year coming up?)
- Net operating income (NOI) or earnings before interest, taxes, depreciation and amortization (EBITDA)
- Funds from operations (FFO)

Study Your Competition

In today's hugely competitive retail environment, remember not to use a narrow delineation of your competition. Your center can lose market share to a wide variety of distribution methods—not just the regional mall down the street. Consider the following competition when completing your analysis:

- neighborhood and community centers
- category killers/power centers
- value-oriented centers
- outlet centers
- discounters
- lifestyle centers
- resale shops
- Internet
- mail order

That being said, in most cases, a superregional center's main source of competition may well be the other superregional center(s) in the market area.

Visit the other centers in your immediate trade area. Study the kinds of stores and the general environment of those centers. How do they compare to yours? Better than? Equal to? Worse than? Observe the shoppers. Ask yourself:

- What stores are they shopping?
- What are they buying?
- What clues suggest their fashion interests? For example, are they carrying designer bags, string bags or nylon backpacks?

You should get to know your competition well and be familiar with its customer profile (where do they live, age, household income, etc). It is also very helpful to know their expansion potential/plans, new leasing deals that are in the works, trade area perceptions about security, price points, amenities, etc. What is their marketing budget compared to your center's? Do they use different marketing strategies?

Core Concepts

✓ SWOT

✓ Competitive advantages and disadvantages

✓ External and internal issues

✓ Problems can sometimes be turned into opportunities

PROBLEMS AND OPPORTUNITIES

So, you've totally analyzed your situation. And you are exhausted—now comes the fun part. Identify problems and opportunities. You organize and interpret the data you've uncovered. What does all this mean to my center?

Review all your information, looking for patterns, challenges and competitive advantages to exploit and expand. Look for major swings in the data. Make a list of the top ten problems and the top ten opportunities for your center. A problem is defined as a negative trend, issue, characteristic or chance for erosion of the center's situation. An opportunity is a trend, issue, characteristic, or chance for progress for the shopping center. Problems and opportunities can also be internal or external. Generally speaking, internal issues can be controlled (the center has no children's apparel offerings and is under-serving the market) and external issues generally cannot be controlled (unemployment is the lowest in 10 years in the market, making it difficult for retailers to find quality sales associates).

It is very important to identify what your center offers that the competition doesn't. Help the consumer recognize the benefits of shopping at your center. Is there one particular advantage you can focus on in your advertising messages? A shopping center's competitive advantage is the factor that sets it apart in the mind of the consumer. This can be the retail offering or center amenities. Analyzing the strengths and weaknesses of your center as it compares to the competition will show you what makes your center different and/or better than others in the area.

Make a list of all the stores in your center and analyze your tenant mix. Compare your list to a list of stores at each competing center. Check for similarities and differences in the retailers represented. You could discover that your center provides a category of stores not found anywhere else in the market area—your competitive advantage. You may also discover a weak merchandise area that needs to be enhanced.

A typical strengths, weaknesses, opportunities and threats (SWOT) exercise is part of step 2 of the marketing plan—defining problems and opportunities. All the data analyzed in step 1 are viewed in the next step in the context of whether they constitute problems or opportunities.

The tenant mix compared to the competition and the trade

area it serves will show strengths and weaknesses. Highlight problem areas and opportunities. Sometimes a problem when defined will offer an opportunity to correct. These can further be addressed in the center's marketing plan in its goals and objectives (step 3), strategies (step 4) and tactics (step 5). Sometimes the solutions to problems lie within other disciplines in addition to marketing. For instance, a void in the center's merchandise mix may require a leasing action to fill that void as well as a marketing action to convey the message to the residents of the trade area. A center's marketing plan addresses problems and opportunities regardless of which discipline must be employed to improve the center's overall productivity.

Core Concepts

✓ Goals and objectives can be addressed through marketing, leasing, development and operational strategies.

✓ Objectives must be specific, achievable, measurable and have a target date for completion.

✓ Enhance center income and value.

GOALS AND OBJECTIVES

The next step in establishing a marketing plan is to set goals and objectives. This is what you want to achieve, but not how you will achieve it. Sometimes several different but related objectives are employed to achieve one goal. Objectives vary widely by center but should be:

- specific
- realistic
- measurable
- have a timeline for completion
- related to enhancing property value and cash flow

The most meaningful marketing goals and objectives relate

back to the center's business plan goals. Set various general goals and specific narrow objectives each year that address each of the problems and opportunities defined in the previous step of the marketing plan. An example of a well-stated goal might be: "To increase the center's average sales per square foot from $350 to $380 and consequently average market rents for total occupancy costs from $35 to $38 per square foot by year end."

To achieve that goal, several underlying objectives may be required. Several examples of well-stated objectives to achieve the previously described goal might be:

1. "To increase average sales per square foot of women's apparel merchants from $390 per square foot to $415 per square foot by year end."
2. "To replace Store A currently performing at $190 per square foot when the lease expires next February with Store B, whose sales potential the first year is $490 per square foot."
3. "To reduce the center's CAM costs from $7 per square foot during the next year to $6.50 per square foot to help increase the center's rent portion of total occupancy costs in new lease deals."

The marketing plan's goals and objectives should include all areas that will enhance the center's productivity. Some will be the end result of marketing, others a combination of marketing and leasing or other disciplines. Examples of objectives that can be addressed exclusively through marketing strategies and tactics are as follows:

1. "To increase pedestrian traffic count averages by year end on Saturdays and Sundays from 22,000 to 25,000."

2. "To increase expenditures by all center customers to food court restaurants from 40 percent to 50 percent by year end."

3. "To increase sponsorship revenue for the center's annual Thanksgiving Day parade next year from $200,000 to $400,000."

4. "To increase awareness of center advertising from a recall of 20 percent to 30 percent of customers in the primary market during the next holiday season compared with the year-before season."

Core Concepts

✓ General directions to reach and motivate the consumer

✓ Center image and general message

✓ Media selection

STRATEGIES

Strategies are the written plan of the methods to be used to achieve the objectives. They convey an approach to supporting the objective. Most strategies include actions like "develop a program" or "create a campaign," and so forth. Tactics are more specific and identify the exact program, the timeline and how much the budget should be. What the customer sees and reacts to is tactical—they don't see the strategic plan.

An example of a strategy to support the objective established above would be:

"Develop a spring fashion campaign to establish XYZ Mall as the fashion authority in the trade area."

Strategies can include media selection such as radio and outdoor to promote to the "9 to 5 worker." Strategies can include the campaign parameters and general message that may vary from various tactical ads.

Strategies can also be directed at the community through community service programs and events. Categories in which the marketing budget is spent are strategies.

Core Concepts

✓ Specific marketing events and advertising

✓ The detailed breakdown of the marketing budget

✓ The calendar of events

TACTICS

Tactics, in a shopping center marketing plan, are driven by the strategies employed. Each strategy would be supported by a series of tactics. For instance, a shopping center whose goal is to connect with the community to generate goodwill might have a strategy of community relations programs and events. The tactic might be to hold a special sale during the first week of October, where charities would sell tickets to the event, thereby raising funds for the charity and increasing sales for the merchant. A second tactic to support the same strategy might be to take a difficult-to-lease store space and turn it into a community room for community groups to hold their meetings.

An example of a tactic to support a public relations strategy to increase the center's fashion image might be:

"Implement a series of press releases to local media during Spring and Fall fashion seasons to promote selection of new styles at key focus retailers."

Core Concepts

✓ Merchants association
✓ Marketing fund
✓ Sponsorship income

THE MARKETING BUDGET

The income utilized in the marketing budget is generated through assessments paid by the tenants and the landlord. Whether the center operates under a merchants' association structure or a marketing/promotion fund, the amount of the assessment is spelled out in the lease document, as follows:

- A merchant's association: This is a not-for-profit, independent corporation with a board of directors who vote and approve the expense budget. The members pay dues. By-laws usually require monthly meetings and an annual report. A center's landlord generally contributes a portion (25% of what the tenants pay) of the association budget and receives voting privileges. There are very few centers still operating under this structure.

- A marketing or promotion fund: This has become a common alternative to the merchants' association structure. It is established through fees paid to the center's landlord. It may have an advisory board to provide tenant input, but the landlord is responsible for all planning, executing and staffing. The tenants have no voting rights. They acknowledge the expertise of the landlord's chosen management and therefore leave the responsibility for marketing in management's hands.

The marketing budget depicts the various forms of revenues as stated above. They can be specialty store assessments, anchor store assessments and landlord contribution. However, other income sometimes flows from alternative revenue sources like "sponsorships" and "partnership marketing." For example, a shopping center may "partner" with a local automobile dealer. The automobile dealer for exposure in the shopping center may provide in-kind product donations, such as a car to be given away, and be required to advertise this shopping center promotional giveaway. The dealer may also be required to contribute a cash amount for this exposure. That income may be shown in the marketing budget as "sponsorship income" or in the shopping center's budget as "other income." In-kind donations do not appear on a marketing budget but are nevertheless tracked by the marketing director.

The expense portion of the marketing budget typically includes media expenses, advertising production, events, and administrative expenses, to name a few.

Core Concepts

✓ Postmortem
✓ Measuring effectiveness
✓ Return on investment (ROI)

FEEDBACK AND DOCUMENTATION

Documentation is very valuable for future planning. Be sure to:

- Make notes as you go along and keep them in a folder (electronic or paper) set up for each event, sale, promotion or campaign.
- Have an organized debriefing program involving as many people as possible. For example, hold a postmortem session soon after an event. Discuss not only what went wrong, but ways to do everything better. Encourage candor by creating an environment in which marketing and operations people feel free to admit less-than-perfect re-

sults and can talk comfortably about how to do better next time.

- Involve as many disciplines as possible and appropriate (manager, maintenance, specialty leasing, etc.).
- Get feedback from your merchants. Did they feel the effort was a success? Did they hear customers comment?
- Get real sales results as compared to last year.

Build a measurement strategy into each marketing effort to help evaluate your success. For example:

- Establish a survey system to be used with your tenants: Make it easy to gather sales statistics in a manner that will allow you to measure changes in sales volume before and after a marketing effort.
- Plan to gather traffic statistics.

Evaluation of Results

Evaluate the effort from every possible aspect. For example:

- Was it the success you wanted?
- Did you get enough "bang for the buck"? Was the result commensurate with funds invested? What was the return on investment (ROI)? How do you know?
- Should it have been longer or shorter; larger or smaller?
- Was the location of the event appropriate?
- Were any outside coordinators or consultants overpaid for what they delivered?
- Was there increased foot traffic?
- Were sales better than they were during the same period last year?

Core Concepts

✓ Tenant orientation
✓ Tenant incentives

TENANT RELATIONS

All the efforts mentioned above will be for naught if you fail to develop and maintain good relations with the tenants in your center. It is vital to marketing success. You are dependent upon the tenants and their willingness to cooperate. Treat them as your partners.

Here are some tactics you can employ.

When a new tenant comes to the center:

- Make it a point to meet the new store manager before the store opens.
- Welcome a new store manager (and owner) personally.

- Invite the store manager to orientation sessions to learn about the center.
- Introduce the new merchant to key tenants. Choose tenants who are good merchants, those who have a positive attitude and are supportive of the landlord and management.

Make an effort to visit with the new store manager/owner three times to establish your relationship early on.

Other things you can do to help maintain good relations with your tenants include:

- Getting to know your merchants and their businesses
- Making frequent personal visits
- Responding promptly to requests for information
- Motivating as many tenants as possible. You may wish to offer small prizes. To motivate tenants and gain their participation in centerwide efforts or meetings, use special incentives on occasion. For example, give a gift certificate at a local restaurant or a weekend getaway at a nearby resort. Prizes for the highest-achieving tenants by sales per square foot in multiple categories encourages a competitive environment and rewards superior performance.
- Being attentive to the high turnover among retail managers, and offering ongoing reeducation programs
- Knowing who the unofficial mall or center "mayor" is, and keeping that person informed and involved
- Working to involve any naysayers and turning them into supporters.

Core Concepts

✓ Marketing plan guides the marketing process
✓ Key measurements

CONCLUSION

Marketing is the process by which you get your "product" into the hands of the consumer. To do this effectively, you must have a marketing plan—a formal written document that defines your shopping center, sets goals and arranges priorities to guide the process in the right direction. The foundation of a marketing plan is research: It provides pertinent information about your area and your consumers. Analyzing your center's attributes and studying your competition will help to determine your competitive advantage—the benefit that draws shoppers to your shopping center instead of someone else's.

Once you have a plan, you need to update it regularly. And

to achieve your marketing goals and objectives, you'll need to implement strategies and tactics. Marketing budgets are funded through assessments, as spelled out in the lease, and may be operated under a merchants' association or a marketing/promotion fund structure.

It's important to build a measurement strategy into each marketing effort and to establish a system of feedback and documentation to evaluate all aspects of your efforts. Finally, a valuable key to marketing success is developing and maintaining good relations with the merchants who are tenants in your center.

Marketing budgets are under pressure to add value to each property. Responsible marketing professionals today assess all marketing programs to be sure sales, overage rental income, traffic, leasing potential, net operating income (NOI) and market share have been improved by their efforts.

Glossary

The glossary that follows is a listing of key definitions compiled from this outline, with several terms not defined in the outline added for your information. The terms are defined within the context of this shopping center management topic.

Advertising plan   A description of the message, themes and creative elements of your advertising campaign. It includes a budget for creative and production services.

"Center mayor"   See "Mall mayor."

Competitive advantage   A benefit—feature, location or concept—that will distinguish your shopping center in the mind of the consumer. A competitive advantage may be real or perceived.

Demographics   Basic objective data about the shoppers in your market area. Demographic statistics include age, gender, household income, education, occupation.

"Mall mayor"   The merchant who is recognized by peers as an informal leader among the shopping center's tenants. This individual is likely to become the spokesperson for the group.

Marketing or promotion fund   Established by a lease-required fee paid to the landlord, this is a pool of monies used to market the center for which shopping center landlords are totally responsible. The fund may have a tenant advisory board. A clause in the lease covers increases in the fee.

Media plan   An outline of the media that you have determined to be most efficient for reaching your target market. It defines exactly which media will be used and when. The plan includes the media-buying budget.

Merchants' association   A not-for-profit, independent corporation with a board of directors who vote and sign checks. The members pay dues. Monthly meetings and an annual report are required.

Partnership marketing   When a shopping center partners with an outside company to pull together funds and resources mutually benefiting each other through the joint efforts. Also known as sponsorships, typical sponsors include an automobile dealer, a credit card company, and a radio station.

Psychographics   An interpretation of lifestyle issues: how people are influenced and what they spend their money on and free time enjoying.

Publicity   Newsworthy information that, when released to the media, will be published or broadcast as news. It is sometimes perceived as free advertising.

Trade area   The geographic boundaries from which your shoppers come.